FOREWORD
BY THE ARCHE

C000173200

Advent is a good tim
deeply hope for, and
purpose for us and fc

This little book invites us to slow down this Advent and take time to look inwards at our hopes and fears; to look outwards at a world in need of hope; and to look God-ward, confident in his love and commitment to the world.

As well as short daily readings, prayers and reflections, we are faced with a challenge (illustrated by an online video) to take a small step towards living more simply and treading more gently through life. To encourage us, the accompanying videos (available at www. readysteadyslow.org.uk) provide inspiring examples of actions churches and individuals have already taken to witness to God's hope.

Archbishop Desmond Tutu summed this up the when he introduced the online version of READY STEADY SLOW in 2009: "For Advent, care for one another; care for our world. It's the only one we have."

It's a great challenge, but one we can approach with great hope.

† Rowan Cantuar:

1 DECEMBER

Today's challenge

Enjoy a green space, take the kids to a playground and breathe in the outdoors.

Reflection

Preparing for something is very important. But it can also become not preparing but anticipating. The excitement of Christmas can pressurize us all (whether children or not) into rushing ahead and by so doing we spoil the actual feast itself.

Although it is very difficult, the message of Advent is for us to slow down and to prepare properly by taking time. All of us can gain in so many ways by taking time to notice what is happening around us rather than rushing headlong to the next thing. As one example of this slowing down we could all try noticing our breathing for even a few moments each day.

Tim Thornton, Bishop of Truro

Reading Matthew 6: 25–34

God gives such beauty to everything that grows in the fields, even though it is here today and thrown into a fire tomorrow. He will surely do even more for you! (Matthew 6:30)

Did you know... ?

On average we breathe in around 22,000 times a day.

Prayer

O God,
open our eyes
to the beauty around us,
open our hearts
to your goodness and generosity,
open our ears
to your call to gratitude and kindness.

Take a look

"Mud between your toes" with the Eden Project and the Bishop of Truro at
www.readysteadyslow.org

2 DECEMBER

Today's challenge
When you turn on the tap, think about those who can't – why not support the work of a development charity?

Reflection
There are two kinds of thirst: physical and spiritual thirst. Physical thirst is relatively easy to assuage (although the tragedy is that there remains far, far too many people in the world who remain unable even to have one drink from a safe source of water). People living in the so-called developed world do not, as a rule, need to worry about physical thirst; what cripples us is spiritual dehydration.

When Jesus speaks in John's gospel about "living water", it is spiritual dehydration that he is talking about. He talks to the woman at the well of a deep down refreshment which comes from the water that only he can give. The image suggested here is of a spring of water that bubbles away constantly. The problem with physical thirst is that one drink simply won't do – we are told at least 8 glasses a day is what we need. If, however, we believe in Jesus then our spiritual hydration is guaranteed far into the future,

constantly renewed and refreshed by the living, bubbling spring within.
**Paula Gooder, Author, Lecturer and
Canon Theologian of Birmingham Cathedral**

Reading John 4: 1–21

Jesus said, "...But no one who drinks the water I give will ever be thirsty again. The water I give is like a flowing fountain that gives eternal life." (John 4: 13a,14)

Did you know... ?

Around one billion people in the world do not have access to safe water.

Prayer

Spirit of God,
water of life,
with joy and hope
you fill our dryness;
and you cause us
to seek life for the deserts
we encounter around us.

Take a look

"Watch your water", featuring a loo–seat petition at
www.readysteadyslow.org

3 DECEMBER

Today's challenge
Pack a bag for life this Advent.

Reflection
When Moses talked about how God's people should relate to the land, he talked about giving the land a rest so that we don't continually drain it of its resources. He also reminded people that the Earth belongs to God and that 'we only live here for a little while.' The fact that we are not here for long should mean that we take care not to cause any lasting damage to the environment.

As Christians we have a moral obligation to lessen the amount of damage that we cause to the environment. But more than that; we are called to represent a God who creates beauty and life and does not harm, destroy or waste.

Roger Morris, Archdeacon of Worcester

Reading Leviticus 25: 18–24

No land may be permanently bought or sold. It all belongs to me – it isn't your land, and you only live there for a little while. (Leviticus 25:23)

Did you know... ?

45% of us have a bag for life but only 18% of us use them (Source: DEFRA).

Prayer

May God's breath cleanse and empower us
May God's strength lead us in times of temptation
May God's guidance help us to seek for alternatives
May God's sensitivity make us tread lightly on creation.
Amen.

Malini Devananda, Sri Lanka

Take a look

Old bags bring new life in Worcester at
www.readysteadyslow.org

4 DECEMBER

Today's challenge
Avoid the tumble dryer – dry clothes on a line whenever you can.

Reflection
Naturally, it's taken me a long time to get around to reading Sten Nadolny's novel **The Discovery of Slowness**.

It's about John Franklin, an Arctic explorer, whose natural pace of living and thinking has been described as that of an elderly sloth after a long massage. But it worked well for him in an environment where more haste would definitely mean less speed.

So it is with the Sun which God decrees to rule the day. Try as we might, there is no way to get it to rise sooner, set later or vary its slow but steady progress across the sky. It has a job to do and it takes just the right amount of time needed to do it. Too slow and we melt; too fast and we freeze.

Instead of wasting energy by going faster than is necessary, let's learn a lesson from the Sun and discover how going slowly can give us all the energy we need. **John Saxbee, Bishop of Lincoln**

Reading Psalm 136: 3–9

He lets the sun rule each day. God's love never fails.
(Psalm 136:8)

Did you know... ?

You can make savings on your electricity bill and 65kg
of CO_2 by drying clothes outside instead of using the
tumble dryer.

Prayer

God our creator,
as the sun brings life
to your fragile world
so may your love
warm our hearts
and release in us
a joyful determination
to tread gently on this earth.

Take a look

"Natural Freebies" at
www.readysteadyslow.org

5 DECEMBER

Today's challenge
Grab a "Sabbath moment" today.

Reflection
Do you remember Sunday?

It used to be a time when the streets were quiet and when there was no shopping, no buying and no spending and families used to eat together.

On a Jewish Sabbath you are not allowed to drive a car, go in a plane, not allowed to switch on electricity. If the whole world kept Sabbath then we would solve the environmental crisis.

Chief Rabbi Jonathan Sacks (speaking at an interfaith forum at Lambeth Palace)

Reading Genesis 2: 1–3

By the seventh day God had finished his work, and so he rested. (Genesis 2:2)

Did you know... ?

There is a wealth of research to prove the health and psychological benefits of children and parents or carers eating together.

Prayer

Eternal God,
present in each moment
of our lives,
help us to rediscover
your gift of rhythm and season;
with your creation
help us to wait,
to rest,
to stop
and so to live
more truly.

Take a look

"Rhythm of Life" contains messages from the Archbishop of Canterbury and the Chief Rabbi.
www.readysteadyslow.org

6 DECEMBER

Today's challenge
Make time to read one of the Psalms – try Psalm 46.

Reflection
The run up to Christmas is busy, busy, busy. All those mince pies to make – all those presents to wrap. And yet, deep down, we know that there has to be more to it than this.

Christmas carols sing to us over the radio and remind of things we learned long ago – shepherds, a stable, angels and wise men. If we can but press the pause button for a moment in the midst of all the busyness, we can focus on what Advent is really all about. It's about preparing to meet the Christ child. That's the best gift of all. The rest is just wrapping.

The aim of Ready Steady Slow is to help us to find that quiet moment in the day – ten minutes on the commuter train or that special silent time when everyone has gone to bed and the house slumbers. The opportunity to carve out a moment to be still and to think about what it might mean – God with us.
Jan McFarlane, Archdeacon of Norwich

Reading Psalm 46

Be still, and know that I am God. (Psalm 46:10a)

Did you know... ?

The shortest Psalm in the Bible is 117 (two verses) and
the longest is 119 (176 verses).

Prayer

O God,
you come to us
in stillness;
and in a silent whisper
you speak words of love
and we, in that moment,
discover the peace
that is eternity.

Take a look

"Refreshing Moments" at
www.readysteadyslow.org

7 DECEMBER

Today's challenge
Take a walk, then take a seat and reflect.

Reflection
We must be the first generation of people who think going on pilgrimage is about arriving rather than travelling. Nowadays, pilgrimage usually means booking a coach for a sort of ecclesiastical sight-seeing tour.

In previous generations it meant travelling somewhere, and usually on foot; and although it was good to have as a destination some sacred site like Canterbury or Walsingham, or even Jerusalem itself, all the benefits one hoped to receive were expected to be found on the road. It was in the "going somewhere", not the "getting somewhere" that truths were revealed; they emerged slowly as the road unfolded.

They are still there to be found by those who dare to slow down to God's pace.
Stephen Cottrell, Bishop of Chelmsford

Reading Psalm 23

...he restores my soul. He guides me in paths of righteousness for his name's sake. (Psalm 23:3)

Did you know... ?

There are more than 140,000 miles of public footpaths in England and Wales.

Prayer

God our rest
thank you for
moments to pause
and places to sit;
help us,
and your world,
to discover
the joy
of your restoration.

Take a look

"Take Your Seat", a church's ministry to walkers complete with compost toilets.
www.readysteadyslow.org

8 DECEMBER

Today's challenge
Look beyond the money, consider the cost of your Christmas.

Reflection
We are told these days that everything has its price and that anything can be bought. But we also discover in life that not everything has value and that balance sheets do not tell us the whole story. As the Beatles recognized: "Money Can't Buy Me Love".

At Christmas we can feel compelled to spend, spend, spend and not think too hard about the cost. Which is why the tinselly dream dies off in January and we are left with the unsparkling bill. But generous living and generous giving can make the world better for many people – whilst also proving more fulfilling to the giver than any amount of "taking" can ever do. Which is what Christmas ultimately is really about.

Generosity is the hallmark of God and should be the most evident characteristic of God's people. But such generosity might mean giving less – and making the less count for more.
Nick Baines, Bishop of Croydon

Reading Isaiah 55: 1–3b

Why waste your money on what really isn't food?
Why work hard for something that doesn't satisfy?
(Isaiah 55:2)

Did you know... ?

£5 buys 50 fruit trees for communities in Ethiopia
(**www.presentaid.org**).

Prayer

God our creator
open our eyes to see
the true value
in all you have made
and open our hearts to receive
the free gift of your
life and love;
turn our greedy consumerism
into generous living.

Take a look

"Priceless" is today's award–winning video by a youth
group from Gillingham, Kent.
www.readysteadyslow.org

9 DECEMBER

Today's challenge
Introduce a new energy-saving initiative where you live and work.

Reflection
How many switches will you use today? Flick, press, turn and change is instant; lights, sounds, images, heat, movement on or off as you choose. It's pretty amazing really. Sometimes, however, it's all too easy, all too quick.

Today, why not pause before you flick the switch. Think about the connections behind it. The energy you use; where it comes from and how it's produced. The effects your choice has on other people, maybe thousands of miles away or maybe next door. Think about the difference that small action might make.

And why not pause and think about change that is life giving and lasting. What might make a real difference in your life, in your community, in your world? It probably won't come in an instant or simply by pressing a button; it's much more likely to be a journey. But it begins with a choice, your choice. What might it mean for you today to choose life?

John Kiddle, Mission Development Officer St Albans

Reading Deuteronomy 30: 19–20
Choose life! (Deuteronomy 30:19b)

Did you know... ?
The average house can save £37 a year by turning off electric appliances rather than leaving them on standby.

Prayer
Jesus,
you chose to walk the way of love
whatever it cost;
in the decisions we make
give us the wisdom to see,
and the courage to choose,
the things which bring life
to others
and to ourselves.

Take a look
"Make the Switch" is today's high action, low energy film from Gloucester.
www.readysteadyslow.org

10 DECEMBER

Today's challenge

Cut your carbon for the sake of the poor – sign up to the Church of England's Climate Justice Fund (**www.climatejusticefund.org**).

Reflection

Jesus told a parable about a widow who kept nagging a judge and asking for justice, she gave the judge such a headache that even though he wasn't really interested in her problems he gave her justice.

The parable is about whether God will find justice on the face of this earth – today there are still widows and orphans suffering injustice, climate injustice. What do I mean by that? Those of us who have the power to do something about it don't really feel the effect of climate change and those who are feeling the effects don't have the power to change the world. The truth is we can begin to take power into our own hands which is exactly what we've done by setting up the Climate Justice Fund – you can do something about the inequity and contribute.

James Jones, Bishop of Liverpool

Reading Micah 6: 1–8

The LORD God has told us what is right and what he demands: "See that justice is done, let mercy be your first concern, and humbly obey your God." (Micah 6:8)

Did you know... ?

In north east Uganda families regularly survive eating wild fruits and seeds when the expected rains do not arrive.

Prayer

Dear Lord,
Please help us remember the birth of Christ this Christmas. Please help people who are less fortunate than us, and those who are facing famine and drought. Please clear the world from illness and wars. Please guide the people who are struggling to survive. Please help the people who have been forced into poverty. Let the Light of the World, Jesus, guide the planet to become a safer place. Amen.

A prayer for the World by James Orledge
(Sarum St Paul's CE VA Primary School, Salisbury)

Take a look

Why "Climate Justice"? Bishop James Jones explains at
www.readysteadyslow.org

11 DECEMBER

Today's challenge
Take a go-slow coffee break or a time-out lunch.

Reflection
Many people today live their lives at such a fast pace that stress, over-work and exhaustion seem to be endemic to our culture. The solution that some find is to look back nostalgically to a time when life was slower, less pressured and consequently less stressful. The implication of this is that if only we could live our lives more like that then we would be less stressed.

This may well be true but the frequent references to Jesus' need to withdraw and pray in the gospels suggest that it is not just living slowly that will help us. Jesus' life in the 1st century would have been lived at the slower pace of an agricultural society and yet he still needed time to withdraw, be alone and to pray.

If Jesus needed time to do this, how much more does each one of us need to take the time to be on our own and to place ourselves in the presence of God?
Paula Gooder

Reading Mark 1: 32–39

Very early the next morning, Jesus got up and went to a place where he could be alone and pray. (Mark 1:35)

Did you know... ?

The Health and Safety Executive report that hundreds of thousands of people in Britain believe they are experiencing work-related stress at a level that is making them ill. (Source: HSE)

Prayer

O God of the desert
and the dawn;
amidst the strident noises
and dazzling glare
in our lives
help us to find a place
quiet enough to hear
your voice
and dark enough to see
your light.

Take a look

Enjoy a short "Workplace Meditation" at
www.readysteadyslow.org

12 DECEMBER

Today's challenge

Support a community project on your doorstep –
be inspired by today's video.

Reflection

What does it take for us to move from being inspired
to getting involved? In an age of information-overload
we're bombarded with inspiring organizations all
seeking our involvement. It's easy to give without
commitment or to retreat into our shells to avoid being
overwhelmed and end up committed to nothing.

But there's a different sort of inspiration: not about
smart presentation and skilful manipulation, but an
irrepressible spring of water bubbling up from deep
within. This tends to come from putting down deep
roots in a local place – being committed to a local
community and to the ecology that undergirds it –
consciously becoming part of an ecosystem rather
than existing as a transient parasite upon it. Perhaps
it's only when we immerse ourselves in this way that
we can find the inspiration to bring about sustainable
transformation. We need to get involved in order to
get inspired. God's words to a restless people in exile

in Babylon: "Settle there and build houses. Plant gardens and eat what you grow in them." (Jeremiah 29:5)
Dave Bookless, Director of A Rocha UK

Reading Isaiah 35: 1-2

Deserts will bloom everywhere and sing joyful songs. (Isaiah 35:2)

Did you know... ?

A growing number of organizations like **www.arocha.org** have a mileage expense allowance for cyclists.

Prayer

As a flower blossoms in the desert, resilient, fragile, vibrant; so may your life, God, flower in our lives, in our communities and in the world.

Take a look

"Community Conscious" features two inspiring stories from London churches. **www.readysteadyslow.org**

13 DECEMBER

Today's challenge
Make a spiritual decision this Christmas.

Reflection
In a world of instant gratification, to ask people to wait is not an easy thing to do. A credit card used to be advertised as "taking the waiting out of wanting". Of course, living through a long recession we now know what happens when we believe that sort of seductive nonsense.

Advent is about learning to wait – not rushing around and jumping to conclusions. It's about not trying to do everything now, but waiting, watching, praying and seeing – all things that appear to be alien to our culture of 'having everything we want when we want it'.

I think if we dare to use Advent wisely, we learn to slow down and to wait and to ask questions like: who is this Jesus who is coming? What do we make of him? What does he want from me?

And after the waiting time there does come a time of decisions. The challenge to all of us is what are we going to do about the Jesus who comes at Christmas?
Nick Baines

Reading Luke 3: 7–18

John told them, "If you have two coats,
give one to someone who doesn't have any. If you have
food, share it with someone else." (Luke 3:11)

Did you know... ?

An average Briton spends 45 hours
a year on hold on the phone.

Prayer

Jesus our Light,
as we prepare to celebrate your birth
may we hear your call
to live rightly,
honestly and generously
and so receive you,
the prince of peace.

Take a look

Bishop Nick Baines talks about
"Waiting Expectantly" at
www.readysteadyslow.org

14 DECEMBER

Today's challenge
Use the leftovers, grow your own compost.

Reflection
As gardeners know, if you want your garden to flourish, you need to spend time digging and preparing the soil in advance. Only by careful preparation, will the seeds we sow take root and flourish.

Advent is similarly a special time of preparation. In it, God calls us to prepare for the coming of his Son into the world. We get ready by slowing down, keeping moments of stillness as we listen to the Father's heartbeat of love as well as his commanding voice. By meditating on Holy Scripture, we give ourselves the opportunity to examine our lives and to respond to God's invitation: follow me. In this way, we prepare ourselves so that Jesus may take root in us.

So this Advent, let us ask for God's grace to prepare for the coming of his Son, Jesus Christ, that his living word may plenteously bear the fruit of the Holy Spirit.
Dr John Sentamu, Archbishop of York

Reading Matthew 13: 1–23

The seeds that fell on good ground are the people who hear and understand the message. They produce as much as a hundred or sixty or thirty times what was planted. (Matthew 13:22)

Did you know... ?

Every tonne of food waste prevented has the potential to save 4.2 tonnes of CO_2 equivalent.

Prayer

God of life
among the hardness,
the shallowness,
the crowdedness
may your words
find a patch of good soil
in which to take root
and grow
and be fruitful.

Take a look

TV presenter Philippa Forrester shows you how to "grow your own" compost in "Rubbish? WRAP" (We would like to thank WRAP for supplying this video – find out more at **www.recyclenow.com/compost**).
www.readysteadyslow.org

15 DECEMBER

Today's challenge
Find somewhere different to reflect and pray.

Reflection

Not all of us are good at sitting still. Sometimes this can lead us to conclude that contemplative prayer is not our thing. But surely all prayer must end, not with our talking to God, but our resting in God's presence, our listening to the stillness of God's voice within us?

So how do the fidgety and the restless find peace? Well, there is a kind of stillness that is found in activity. For many of us the body needs to be kept busy so that the spirit can rest. This is why posture is always important in prayer. It is also why walking, or, for some, running, or going on pilgrimage, or slowly winding your way round a labyrinth, or marking the stations of the cross lead to an inner restfulness and an inner waiting upon God.

Stephen Cottrell

Reading Psalm 84

You bless all who depend on you for their strength and all who deeply desire to visit your temple. (Psalm 84:5)

Did you know... ?

There are many public mazes in the UK, from the historic hedge maze at Hampton Court to the water maze at Hever Castle and the Peace Maze in Northern Ireland.

Prayer

God our companion,
on the journeys we make today,
open our eyes to see
open our ears to listen
open our hearts to love
and help us
to pause
and to know
that you are
alongside us.

Take a look

Follow an Oxford prayer maze and reflect with the Quiet Garden movement in "Pray As You Go" at
www.readysteadyslow.org

16 DECEMBER

Today's challenge
Make one fewer fuel-filled journey each day.

Reflection
Most of us will be travelling today; going to work, on the school run, popping out to the shops... For many it can be a cramped, frustrating experience. More often than not our travelling is simply about getting to our destination as quickly as possible; it can feel like lost time. A recent headline stated "UK commuters waste 4.6 million hours a day".

A journey, like Advent itself, is an opportunity, for discovery, for seeing and hearing new things, for listening, for prayer and reflection, for conversation and companionship. It has the potential to surprise. A journey is not wasted time, it's a gift.

So, if you possibly can, slow down and enjoy the journey.
John Kiddle

Reading Luke 24: 13–15
Jesus came near and started walking along beside them. (Luke 24:15)

Did you know... ?
Domestic transport is the source of around 24% of all domestic CO_2 emissions in the UK?

Prayer
Christ the stranger
who walked alongside
friends in their sorrow
and shared
their bread,
give us grace
to walk
with others on
their journeys
and so become
true companions.

Take a look
"Cut the Car" and take
a ride on the new community rickshaw
scheme in Suffolk at
www.readysteadyslow.org

17 DECEMBER

Today's challenge
Make your parties paperless this Christmas.

Reflection
It's no accident that Jesus' first miracle took place at a wedding feast. It would have been very embarrassing indeed for the families of the bride and groom if the wine had run out. So Jesus turns water into wine. Not just the odd bottle or two – but gallons of the stuff. God loves a party!

This first miracle, recorded for us in John's Gospel (John 2:1–10) shows us that, above all, our God is a God of abundant generosity. God loves to give. And his greatest act of generous love was to die in our place on the cross that first Easter.

God loves it when his people mirror his generosity. The verses from Isaiah in today's reading encourage us to be God-like in the way we live our lives. And not only are we to give abundantly, but we are to be generous to others in the way in which we live our lives. If we're selfish, others suffer. If we live generously and thoughtfully, others can know life in all its fullness.
Jan McFarlane

Reading Isaiah 58: 6–9

Share your food with everyone who is hungry; share
your home with the poor and homeless. Give clothes
to those in need; don't turn away your relatives.
(Isaiah 58:7)

Did you know... ?

Some paper products can take up
to five years to decompose.

Prayer

The prayer of St Teresa of Avila

Christ has no body on earth
but yours, no hands but
yours, no feet but yours;
yours are the eyes through
which to look with Christ's
compassion on the world, yours
are the feet with which he is to go about doing
good, and yours are his hands with which to bless us
now.

Take a look

"Paperless Parties" includes advice on making your
parties paperless and other seasonal tips from the
Anglican Diocese of Europe.
www.readysteadyslow.org

18 DECEMBER

Today's challenge
Ponder the planet and make a lifestyle pledge.

Reflection
Advent is an opportunity to open our eyes. Whether at home or at work; Advent invites us to take another look. Often our busyness and the rush of life prevent us seeing the really important things right in front of us. Here are two suggestions:

Take time today to open your eyes to the beauty around you. Pause to see something wonderful in even the small and familiar. Stop to reflect and in gratitude recognize your dependence on the joyful provision of God.

Take time today to open your eyes to the effects of the changing climate around the world. Pause to see how those hardest hit are those who are least able to adapt and least to blame for it. Stop to reflect and in justice recognize your need to live more simply and more generously.

We live in a wonderful world. Be thankful and make it more wonderful by sharing the good things that God gives.
John Kiddle

Reading Genesis 1

God looked at what he had done, and it was good.
(Genesis 1:31)

Did you know... ?

Washing clothes at 30°C uses up to 40% less energy
than higher temperatures.

Prayer

Help us O God
to see,
to enjoy,
and to treasure
this wonderful world
which you have made
and, O God,
help us so to live
on this earth
that its goodness and beauty
may be shared
and not destroyed.

Take a look

"What a wonderful world" is the theme of today's
video from the Diocese of St Albans at
www.readysteadyslow.org

19 DECEMBER

Today's challenge
Mind the gap in your curtains, lag your loft.

Reflection
There are so many simple things we do everyday that if only we took the time to stop and think – "Is there a better way?" we could well make little changes that when added together could make a real difference. And when there is, maybe we find it's an opportunity to change a habit of a lifetime. Drawing the curtains just a little earlier each day in the winter could mean a room needs less heating later that evening. How many other simple changes around our homes would make our living more efficient?

The Church of England has its own Shrinking the Footprint campaign which encourages saving energy across its 16,000 parish churches. A simple adjustment to a time switch or changing to more efficient equipment would make a big saving on all the energy used. You will find lots of suggestions on **www.shrinkingthefootprint.org** and if you can suggest something your church has done which you would

recommend to others do let the organizers know – no matter how simple it may be.
David Shreeve, the Church of England's national environment adviser

Reading Psalm 89

Our LORD, you bless those who join in the festival and walk in the brightness of your presence. (Psalm 89:15)

Did you know... ?

More than 25% of the heat in your home could be escaping through the roof. Take a look at Grants at a glance **www.government-grants.co.uk**.

Prayer

O God, whose glory was seen in the poverty of a stable, help us to choose today to live simply, and so may your light shine more brightly in our hearts and in the world.

Take a look

"Curtain Call" features insulation tips from a project in Newcastle and Durham Dioceses.
www.readysteadyslow.org

20 DECEMBER

Today's challenge
What are you good at? Use a God-given talent today,
wherever you are.

Reflection
In life each of us is dealt a different hand; we are each
given a different set of talents, opportunities, gifts,
passions and circumstances. We shouldn't spend our
life wishing we were someone else, but live our lives to
the full by trying to make the very best of what we have
been given. This is what to means live after the mind
and likeness of Christ. It means accepting and rejoicing
in the gifts and opportunities we have been given.
It means becoming the person we are meant to be.

At the end of my life, God isn't going to say to me, "Why
weren't you the Archbishop of Canterbury?" or "Why
weren't you Barack Obama?", or "Why weren't you St
Francis of Assisi?" but "Why weren't you Stephen?"
Stephen Cottrell

Reading Matthew 25: 14–30

"Wonderful!" his master replied. "You are a good and faithful servant. I left you in charge of only a little, but now I will put you in charge of much more. Come and share in my happiness! (Matthew 25:23)

Did you know... ?

Churchgoers overall contribute 23.2 million hours voluntary service each month in their local communities outside the church.

Prayer

Jesus,
you fed hungry people
with a boy's picnic;
help us to put into your hands
the skills and time,
the love and passion
that you have given us
and in this risky, joyful act of faith
bring life to your world.

Take a look

Watch Stephen Cottrell's invitation to "Be Yourself" at
www.readysteadyslow.org

21 DECEMBER

Today's challenge
Enjoy a carol service this Christmas.

Reflection
"Hark! The herald Christians – and everyone else – sing..." At Christmas we are all at it: huge numbers of people gather in churches, cathedrals, homes and even pubs to sing the well-remembered carols.

Christmas carols try to put into words what is almost impossible to express: that God has come among us as one of us and is on our side. They attempt to explore the mystery of God – in Jesus of Nazareth – opting into the world and not exempting himself from it. We can sing about it for ever, but we also need to dare to think about what it means.

Carols are wonderful attempts to re-tell the familiar story of how God entered our world – not on a war-horse or in a tank, but in a vulnerable baby in occupied territory in a place of weakness. And this is how God decides to be "with us", Emmanuel.

No wonder the angels could begin their song – addressed to ordinary people like us – with simple

words in a complex world: "Don't be afraid!"
Nick Baines

Reading Luke 2: 8–16
But the angel said, "Don't be afraid! I have good news for you, which will make everyone happy." (Luke 2:10)

Did you know... ?
39% of the population attend a Christmas service of some sort.

Prayer
Jesus,
your birth is celebrated
in the music of heaven
and the carols of earth;
in our joy and laughter
give us ears to hear the angels'
song and seek peace and
good will for all people.

Take a look
Sing along with beach hut carols in "On the Beach" at
www.readysteadyslow.org

22 DECEMBER

Today's challenge
Slow down on the roads this Christmas.

Reflection
There's an old prayer for motorists which some Christians pray each time they start the engine of their car. One of the lines reads, "Teach me to use my car for others need; nor miss through love of undue speed, the beauty of the world; that thus I may with joy and courtesy go on my way."

If everyone drove that way – mindful of the needs of others – just imagine what a different experience travelling on our roads would be.

"Love your neighbour as yourself" must be one of the most well known of Jesus' sayings. And perhaps one of the hardest to live up to. Sometimes it's easy to be overwhelmed by the extent of the needs of others. But while as one person you may not be able to change the world, you can certainly change the world for one person. As the late Anita Roddick, founder of the Body Shop, once said, "If you think you're too small to be effective, you haven't been in bed with a mosquito."
Jan McFarlane

Reading Mark 12: 28-31

The second is this: "Love your neighbour as yourself."
There is no commandment greater than these."
(Mark 12:31)

Did you know... ?

Two out of three accidents where people
are killed or injured happen on roads
where the speed limit is 40 mph
or less.

Prayer

God of justice,
help us not to be overwhelmed
by the size of the needs around
us
nor deaf to the cries for help
but give us
compassion to listen
courage to act
and the commitment
to make a lasting difference.

Take a look

Help your neighbour with the Generous
Scheme in "Watch Your Speed".
www.readysteadyslow.org

23 DECEMBER

Today's challenge

Find out what the Mothers' Union really does at home and abroad.

Reflection

"He never spoke a word to me about being a Christian. It was not his words or his preaching but it was just Livingstone that won me for Christ. I was not a Christian when I found him but I had not been with him very long before I was worshipping Livingstone's God, trusting his Saviour, and reading his Bible."

These remarkable words were written by Henry Morton Stanley in his diary a few months after meeting the missionary and explorer David Livingstone in November 1871.

They witness powerfully to the beauty and transforming impact of a Christian life lived for others, and a desire to bring God's word and God's justice to the world. The Mother's Union is at the heart of this, especially in Africa. God's word in the Bible translated into the languages people speak, and God's word in action, translated into the lives that people lead: is there a more powerful combination?

Stephen Cottrell

Reading Matthew 5: 1–16

God blesses those people who want to obey him more than to eat or drink. They will be given what they want! (Matthew 5:6)

Did you know... ?

The MU has 3.6 million members working in more than 78 countries, and even has a Facebook group.

Prayer

O God, we thank you for the fullness of this season, for food and warmth, for companionship and celebration; give us also we pray the gift of hunger, that we may long for justice and peace and find in you and your ways our true fulfilment.

Take a look

"Right to Read" shows the Mother's Union in action.
www.readysteadyslow.org

24 DECEMBER
CHRISTMAS EVE

Today's challenge
What are **you** waiting for? Give it some thought.

Reflection
Many of us rush through Christmas Day in a flash of
mince pies, wrapping paper and children playing.
So much so, in fact that when we get to the end
of Christmas Day we end up feeling we've missed
something.

Advent teaches us to wait and be fully present in the
moment right now that God has given to us. It also
teaches us to train our eyes on the horizon so that we
can look for glimmers of God's presence in the world.
In these glimmers we can see the world, not as it is
now, but as God yearns for it to be: a world no longer
troubled by sorrow, pain and disillusionment but filled
with the glorious love of God.

May we hold on to this vision throughout the season of
Christmas that is almost upon us – and onwards into a
joyful, peaceful God–filled New Year.
Paula Gooder